A BRIEF HISTORY of UNDERPANTS

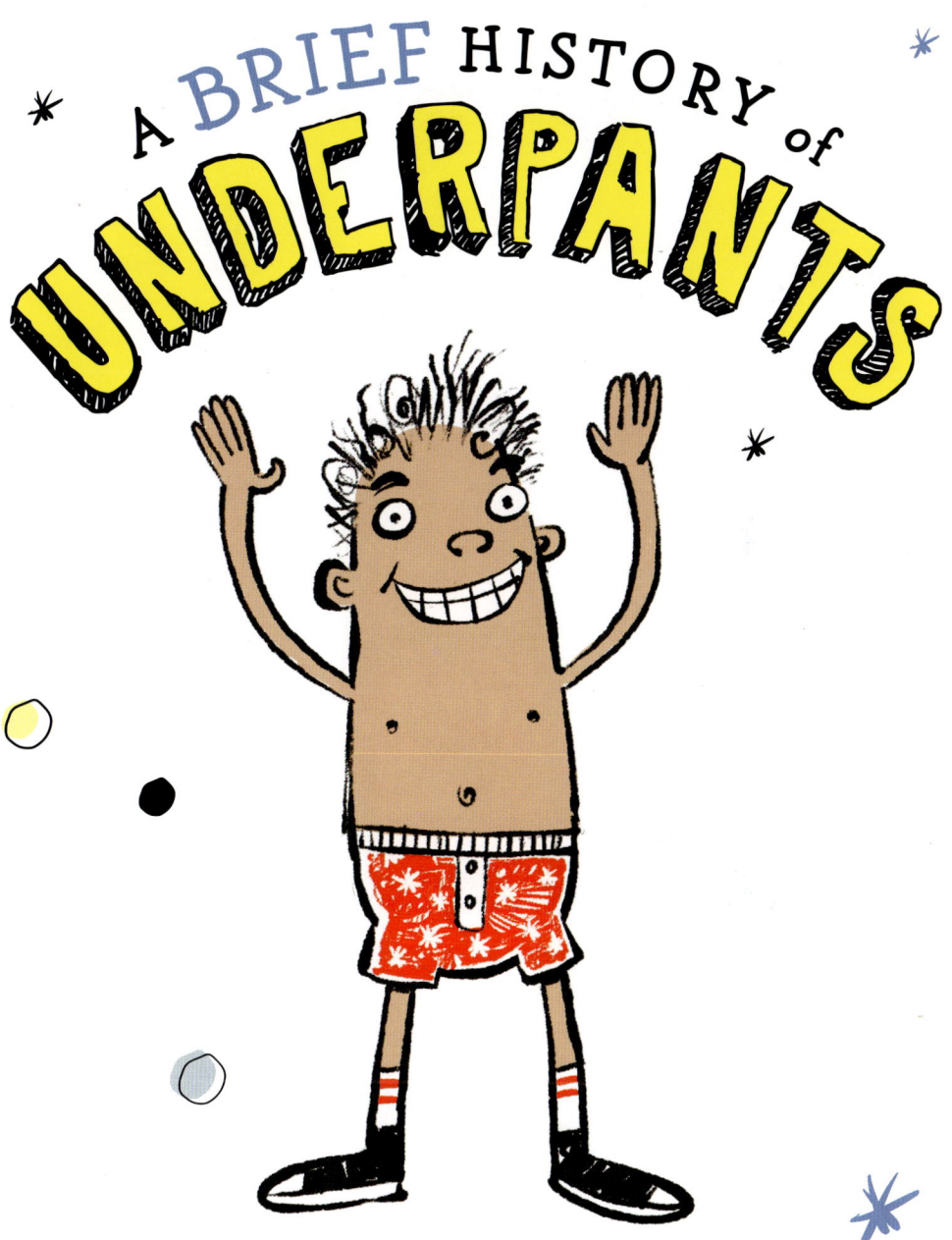

Written by CHRISTINE VAN ZANDT
Illustrations BY HARRY BRIGGS

becker&mayer! kids

For my clever, imaginative daughter, my supportive husband, my editing cat, and my father—who was right. For my workshop friends, the Fab Five: it took The Village. —CVZ

Brimming with creative inspiration, how-to projects, and useful information to enrich your everyday life, Quarto Knows is a favorite destination for those pursuing their interests and passions. Visit our site and dig deeper with our books into your area of interest: Quarto Creates, Quarto Cooks, Quarto Homes, Quarto Lives, Quarto Drives, Quarto Explores, Quarto Gifts, or Quarto Kids.

© 2021 Quarto Publishing Group USA Inc.

Published in 2021 by becker&mayer! kids, an imprint of The Quarto Group, 11120 NE 33rd Place, Suite 201, Bellevue, WA 98004 USA.
www.QuartoKnows.com

becker&mayer! kids titles are also available at discount for retail, wholesale, promotional, and bulk purchase. For details, contact the Special Sales Manager by email at specialsales@quarto.com or by mail at The Quarto Group, Attn: Special Sales Manager, 100 Cummings Center Suite 265D, Beverly, MA 01915 USA.

21 22 23 24 25   5 4 3 2 1

ISBN: 978-0-7603-7060-5

Digital edition published in 2021
eISBN: 978-0-7603-7061-2

Library of Congress Cataloging-in-Publication Data available upon request.

Author: Christine Van Zandt
Illustrator: Harry Briggs

Printed, manufactured, and assembled in China, 2/21.

338086

CONTENTS

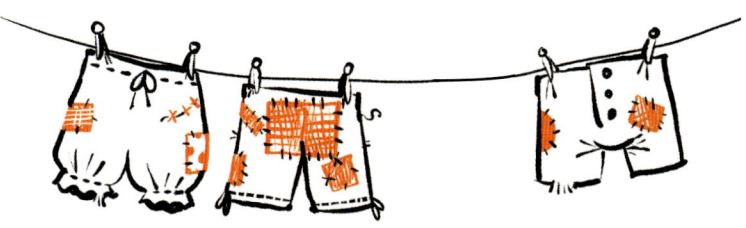

CHAPTER 1

CRUSTY OLD BUNS

What is it about underpants that **CRACKS** us up?

How long has underwear been **UNDER THERE**?

What's **BEHIND** today's styles?

Who started the whole **HOLE** thing?

Let's take a peek at what tushes around the world were wearing on all seven continents!

HERE'S A BRIEF HISTORY...

Since the beginning of buns, people have needed protection from spiky plants, curious bugs, and the weather. They invented styles of underpants using natural plant and animal materials.

Scientists discover
evidence of old undies
the same way they
dig up dinosaur fossils.
New finds are unearthed
all the time.

Ice Bridge, Asia and North America

20,000 -10,000 BCE

In cold places, people layer clothing. Early ancestors of the Inuit stayed warm by wearing underpants made of caribou skin with the fur facing inward. Over that, they wore another layer with the fur facing outward.

ÖTZI THE ICEMAN

Europe

3300 BCE

Mountain climbers in the icy Alps discovered a frozen man with bits of clothing left, including his 5,300-year-old sheepskin loincloth.

CHAPTER 2

UNDERPANTS AROUND THE WORLD

Not all underpants look the same.
From Bali to Belgium to Brazil,
different societies have worn different
things on their behinds.

EGYPT

1324 BCE

Schenti

On ancient Egyptians' humble heinies were rough, dull-colored loincloths. **King Tut**'s royal rear was covered with a fancy, silky one.

Because this famous Egyptian pharaoh believed in life after death, he was buried with **145 pairs of underpants**. No one wants to be stuck doing laundry in the afterlife.

Ancient Egyptians made awesome red dye. Today's experts have tried figuring out how it was done back then. Here's their recipe:

1. Soak thread in **Sheep poop** and rotten olive oil

2. Dry for six months

3. Wear proudly in this life and the next

13

JAPAN

20 - present

Japan's sumo wrestlers competed nearly naked in unwashed mawashi. Washing weakened the fabric and was considered bad luck.

mawashi

Unrolled mawashi are about as long as a school bus and as heavy as a large watermelon. When mawashi come apart during the competition, the wrestler is disqualified, and that's a wrap.

EXTRA!
Learn how to dress like a samurai on **page 44.**

MONGOLIA

1200 - 1350

The Mongols also didn't believe in washing their clothing. **Genghis Khan**'s horseback-riding army wore tightly woven silk under-armor. When a Mongol was shot with an arrow, his silk undershirt wrapped around the arrowhead keeping it from piercing the skin—really important for those poison-tipped arrows.

EUROPE

1000 to 1500

Knights wore quilted, padded underpants.
Horseback riding could be rough and bouncy.
A cushioned tush felt better, gave extra
protection, and kept chain mail from rubbing.

Women, including damsels in distress, wore undergarments that looked like long nightgowns. Beneath, their bottoms were bare. They didn't need padded protection like warriors. A woman's biggest battle was fought once or twice a year on Wash Day.

17

EUROPE

476 - 1453

Without running water, people in Medieval Europe had a hard time getting clean. Because they didn't know about germs yet, some avoided bathing because they thought it would make them sick. Underclothing kept a bit of body odor from getting on their outer layers.

Ye Olde River

ASH

Pee

Lice and fleas like unwashed clothing.

Wash Day was an awful chore. Soaking clothes in ashes mixed with pee helped remove stains, brighten colors, and degrease spots. Those heavy presoaked clothes were then dragged to the river and scrubbed with pebbles or beaten on rocks.

19

maxtlatl

CENTRAL + SOUTH AMERICA

The Maya: 250 - 900, The Inca: 1200 - 1525,
The Aztecs: 1345 - 1521

These three great civilizations wore cotton
or wool loincloths, sometimes with a tunic.
Since it was warm in Mexico and Central and
South America, they didn't wear much else.

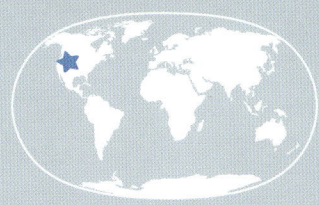

NORTH AMERICA

1400 - 1850

Native Americans wore breechcloths made of tanned deerskin, cloth, or animal fur. Just like we have lots of words for underpants, they did too: breechclout, lionskin, skin clout, and flap.

You could tell a person's age or social status by the fabric, style, and decorations on their loincloth. Each empire had rules about this. Designs, embroidery, feathers, or fringe were only allowed for the most important men.

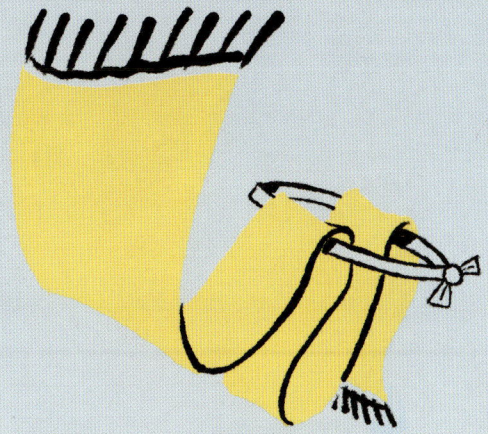

21

apron

AUSTRALIA

1700 - 1900

Down Under, they wore aprons down under. The First Nations people of Australia made string aprons out of human hair and animal fur. An apron's colors showed age and rank.

maro

NEW ZEALAND

1400 - 1870

The maros worn by New Zealand's First Nation people, the Māori, declared someone's importance. A chief's daughter could wear bright-green-feathered parrot skin, but a common person's maro was made of plain wood hen skin..

23

MALI
700 - 1645

In Mali, girls wore small leather-paneled underclothes. Once they were older, they switched to an underpants skirt. The woven patterns and fringe were made from baobab tree bark because, when it comes to underpants, the baobab tree is all bark and no bite.

INDIA

1920 - 1948

To strip away the power Britain had over India, **mahatma Gandhi** stripped down to his dhoti. Making and wearing traditional handspun clothing was a form of protest that helped India gain independence from British rule.

dhoti

CHAPTER 3

CHEEKY INVENTIONS

Before the Industrial Revolution, you couldn't buy new underpants. You had to make them. There were no shopping malls, and forget about ordering **online**: the only **line** underpants were **on** was the clothesline.

Buttons
Pakistan 3000 BCE

5000 BCE 3000 2000 1000 1000 1100 1200 1300 AD

Buttonholes
Germany 13th century

Just like peanut butter and jelly were meant to be together, so were buttons and buttonholes. However, the first buttons made had to wait around over four thousand years before meeting their other halves, the buttonholes.

safety pins

ROMANS 27 BCE - 700 CE

Some inventions were lost when one civilization ended and another began. The Romans used a safety pin, which was forgotten for over a thousand years before being patented in the United States in 1849.

COTTON GIN

U.S.A. 1793

The cotton gin was invented to quickly separate cotton fibers from seeds. This machine began the mass production of cotton yarns and fabrics.

SEWING MACHINE
England 1790

The sewing machine produced clothing faster than hand sewing. Once clothing factories started up, underpants bought at stores (called ready-mades) replaced home-sewn pairs.

ELASTIC

ELASTIC WEBBING 1820

VULCANIZED RUBBER 1836

With a streeetch of the imagination, elastic webbing and rubber were invented. Going to the bathroom no longer required untying complicated bows. Now you could pull down your underpants and go!

IN 1935, when the y-front brief was invented, boys didn't even have to pull down their underpants anymore to go Number One. They just moved the material to the side.

LYCRA 1950

NYLON 1939

Y-FRONT BRIEF 1935

Next came nylon, the world's first man-made fabric, and Lycra, a fabric that could be stretched without losing its shape. These materials were perfect for form-fitting undies.

33

BLOOMERS
U.S.A. 1851

Amelia Jenkins Bloomer popularized bloomers in America in 1851. Before that, women wore layers of underclothes to help protect outer clothing from sweat and body odors.

Say NO to CORSETS

During the 1800s, people thought it was impolite to talk about underclothing. It was nicknamed "unmentionables."

AUTOMATIC WASHING MACHINE
U.S.A. 1937

Because of indoor plumbing, underpants could be washed more easily and more often, making Wash Day less of a battle. Cleaner underclothing meant healthier people.

CHAPTER 4

TUSHES TODAY WORLDWIDE

1980s TO NOW

Now, underpants come in all shapes, styles, and sizes. They even have their own holiday in the USA, National Underpants Day, celebrated on August 5th!

Every year, Kona, Hawaii, has an underpants run, and New York hosts a No Pants Subway Ride.

ANTARCTICA

2018

American endurance athlete Colin O'Brady was the first person to cross the frozen continent of Antarctica on foot without help. Because he had to pull everything he packed, he only brought the underpants on his tush.

He accidentally pooped his only pair of underpants, and 38 days later, Colin and his skid mark made history.

SPACE

International Space Station

2003 - present

An astronaut's dirty underpants are sent back to Earth on a crew-less ship and burn up on reentry. Be careful wishing on that shooting star—it might be flaming underpants.

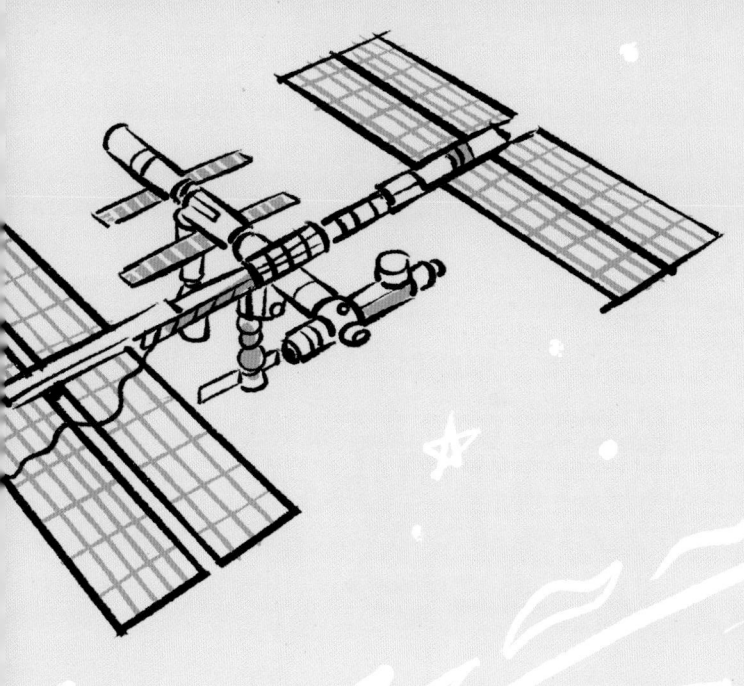

During launch, reentry, and space walks, astronauts
put on long underpants with adult diapers—just in case.
Without a laundromat on the International Space
Station, astronauts wear their pairs for up to a week.

Around the world, underpants have been a part of our history. Whether using fur or feathers, bark or leather, people have found a way to cover up. Inventions and factories propelled our bottoms into the future.

Today, underpants are everywhere. We laugh when characters in books and movies dare to bare their no-longer "unmentionables."

The bottom line:

Underpants are no longer a topic kept under wraps!

THE ENDS.

43

EXTRAS

JAPAN

700 - present

MAKE YOUR OWN FUNDOSHI

Samurai warriors wore fundoshi, which was made from a long strip of cloth. Here's how to dress like a samurai. Ask an adult for help.

SUPPLIES

- Fabric, such as an old twin-size sheet or pillowcase
- Scissors (with adult supervision)
- A measuring tape

STEP 1: MAKING THE BELT

Measure around your waist and write down that number. Cut a belt as long as your waist measurement PLUS another twelve inches.

STEP 2: MAKING THE UNDERPANTS

The fabric will be HALF as wide as the length of your waist measurement and FOUR TIMES as long. For example, if your total waist measurement was 20 inches, then cut the fabric 10 inches wide by 40 inches long. Measurements don't need to be exact.

STEP 3:
PUTTING ON YOUR FUNDOSHI

a) Roll the 10-inch edge of the fabric around the middle of the belt 3 or 4 times to secure it.

b) With the fabric covering your buns, tie the belt near your belly button.

c) Bring the fabric between your legs and under the belt, toward your chest.

d) Flip the fabric over the top of the belt. You're ready to have fun in your fundoshi!

JOKES

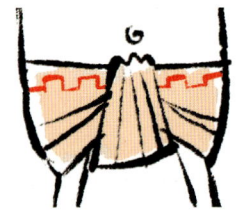

Q. Why does a pirate wear underpants?

A. To hide his booty.

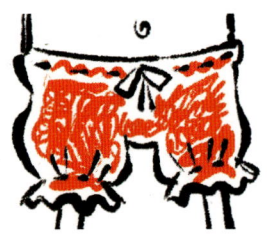

Q. What does a cloud wear under his rain jacket?

A. Thunderwear

FURTHER READING

Bingham, Jane. *A History of Fashion and Costume Volume 1: The Ancient World.* New York: Facts On File, 2005.

Chrisp, Peter. *A History of Fashion and Costume Volume 6: The Victorian Age.* New York: Facts on File, 2005.

Daynes, Katie. *The Revealing Story of Underwear.* London: Usborne Publishing Ltd., 2006.

Elgin, Kathy. *A History of Fashion and Costume Volume 2: Elizabethan England.* New York: Facts On File, 2005.

Kyi, Tanya Lloyd. *50 Underwear Questions: A Bare-All History.* Buffalo: Annick Press, 2011.

Lattimore, Deborah Nourse. *I Wonder What's Under There?: A Brief History of Underwear, A Lift-the-Flap Book.* New York: Harcourt Brace, 1998.

National Geographic Children's Books. *5,000 Awesome Facts (About Everything!) 2.* Washington, D.C: National Geographic Society, 2014.

Rooney, Anne. *A History of Fashion and Costume Volume 5: The Eighteenth Century.* New York: Facts On File, 2005.

Shaskan, Kathy. *How Underwear Got Under There: A Brief History.* New York: Dutton Children's Books, 2007.

Steele, Philip. *A History of Fashion and Costume Volume 2: The Medieval World.* New York: Facts On File, 2005.

Swain, Ruth Freeman. *Underwear: What We Wear Under There.* New York: Holiday House, 2008.

Weber, Paige. *A History of Fashion and Costume Volume 4: Early America.* New York: Facts On File, 2005.

Whitty, Helen. *Underwear.* South Yarra: Macmillan Education Australia, 2000.

About the Author

Christine Van Zandt loves uncovering interesting historical facts that make great books for kids (though she hasn't found any fossilized underpants—yet!). She lives in Los Angeles, California, with her husband, daughter, two cats, and a monarch butterfly sanctuary.

Visit her online at christinevanzandt.com.

About the Illustrator

Harry Briggs has spent the better part of 30 years solving creative riddles for a spectrum of clients including The Quarto Group, Scholastic, McGraw-Hill, Houghton Mifflin Harcourt, *LA Times*, and *The Washington Post*. Harry doodles his days away in the foothills of the Sierra Nevada Mountains with his family and an assortment of woodland creatures that frequent his yard.